Feathery
Creatures

Clint Twist

Author: Clint Twist
Managing Editor: Ruth Hooper
Editor: Emily Hawkins
Art Director: Ali Scrivens
Designer: Bill Mason
Picture Editor: Frances Vargo

Created and produced by
Andromeda Children's Books
An imprint of Pinwheel Ltd
Winchester House
259-269 Old Marylebone Road
London
NW1 5XJ, UK
www.pinwheel.co.uk

Andromeda Children's Books
An imprint of Pinwheel Ltd

ISBN 1-86199-131-2

9 8 7 6 5 4 3 2 1

Printed in China

Contents

Introduction

Harris Hawk

All birds have a covering of feathers that grow from their skin. These feathers are much more than just a body covering. Birds could not survive without their feathers.

DID YOU KNOW?

Birds are not the only warm-blooded animals that can fly. Bats can also fly. Bats are mammals. They have fur, not feathers.

All birds have wings, but some of them, such as ostriches and penguins, cannot fly.

Brent Geese

Feathers In Flight

All birds have wings and most of them are excellent fliers. Some birds, like these geese, fly great distances. During the summer the geese live in the far north, but as winter approaches they fly south for hundreds of miles to warmer climates.

Most birds have long toes with claws.

There are two types of feather on the wings. Large feathers are on the lower part of each wing. Smaller feathers are on the upper part of each wing.

A hawk owl has short feathers on its head and face. They look like thick fur.

Northern Hawk Owl

Hawk Wings

Each of this hawk's wings is larger than the rest of its body. The wings weigh much less than the body because they are mostly made of feathers. Without the feathers, the wings would look very small.

Feathered Family

Feathers keep animals warm. These young hawk owls have their own coats of warm feathers, and they also snuggle up to an adult for extra warmth. The colours and patterns of their feathers help these birds blend in with the background, so predators cannot see them.

FASCINATING FEATHERY FACTS

The wandering albatross has the biggest wingspan of any animal. It measures more than 3 metres (10 feet) across.

Some Arctic terns fly more than 40,000 km (25,000 miles) each year on a round-trip to Australia.

Most feathers have smooth, rounded edges.

Who Is Feathery?

Birds are the only animals that have feathers. There are many different types of bird. Most birds can fly, but some cannot. All birds have one thing in common – they all have feathers.

FASCINATING FEATHERY FACT

There are about 9,000 species of bird in the world.

Many birds can sleep on branches without losing their balance.

Feathered Flocks

Some birds live alone and some live in family groups. Others live in larger groups called *flocks*. During the day, members of the flock may separate to hunt for food. In the evening, the flock gathers again to find a safe place to sleep.

Roosting Birds

Scarlet Macaw

Rainbow Climber

The scarlet macaw is related to the parrot. It lives in hot, wet forests. The macaw is an excellent flier, but spends most of its time climbing through branches in search of fruit. Its feet have flexible toes so it can grip thin branches. The macaw also uses its hooked beak to help it climb.

When the macaw is not using its wings, they are folded flat against its body.

Small, overlapping feathers cover a pigeon's body.

Pigeon

Ground Feeder

Some birds catch insects in mid-air. Others feed on fish. But most birds find their food on the ground or in trees. Birds like this pigeon spend far more time walking on the ground than flying through the air.

Did you Know?

Some birds, such as the macaw, can be taught to copy human speech.

Pigeons and starlings are sometimes thought of as pests, because they eat farmers' crops.

What Are Feathers?

Feathers are flat, lightweight structures that grow from a bird's skin. Each feather has a hollow shaft in the centre with hair-like barbs attached to it.

Ostriches do not have feathers on their necks or legs.

Hatching Ostrich Chick

Newly Hatched

Young birds are known as *chicks*. They hatch from eggs that have thin, hard shells. Some birds, like the ostrich, have feathers that start to grow while they are still inside their eggs. Other chicks are pink and featherless when they hatch. It takes a few days for their first feathers to grow.

When the chick hatches, its feathers are still wet from the fluid inside its egg.

FASCINATING FEATHERY FACTS

Flying birds have four different kinds of feather. Each one serves a special purpose.

The number of feathers a bird has depends on its size and where it lives.

Running Giants

Ostriches are the biggest birds on earth. They have small, stumpy wings and cannot fly, but they are very fast runners. The feathers on an ostrich's wings are very fluffy – they are not shaped for flying.

Long, fluffy feathers stick out from the sides of ostriches' wings.

Ostriches

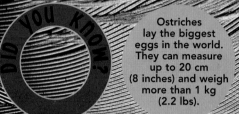

DID YOU KNOW?

Ostriches lay the biggest eggs in the world. They can measure up to 20 cm (8 inches) and weigh more than 1 kg (2.2 lbs).

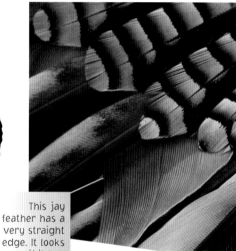

This jay feather has a very straight edge. It looks as if it has been cut.

Jay Wing Feathers

Well-Designed Wings

Every feather on a bird's body is shaped for a particular purpose. This close-up of a jay's wing shows that no two wing feathers have exactly the same shape. In order for the wing to work properly, each feather has to be in exactly the right position.

How Are Feathers Useful?

Birds could not live without feathers. They rely on them for flying, for keeping warm and dry, for camouflage and for signalling to each other.

Hummingbird

The bee hummingbird is the smallest bird in the world. It measures just 6 cm (2¼ inches) – about the size of your finger!

Hummingbirds can flap their wings up and down more than 70 times a second.

The position of each feather can be adjusted to change the shape of the wing.

Winter Warmth

Birds are warm-blooded animals. They must keep their bodies at a constant warm temperature. Feathers provide a layer of *insulation*. This is a barrier that stops body heat from being lost, so birds, like this robin, can stay warm during the coldest winters.

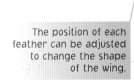

Tightly packed feathers protect the robin from cold winter temperatures.

European Robin

FASCINATING · FEATHERY FACTS ·

Only the male robin has bright red feathers on its chest – female robins have plain, brown feathers.

A turkey chick can eat more than 4,000 insects a day.

Small feathers give a hummingbird's body a smooth outline.

Hovering Hummingbirds

Birds fly by flapping their feather-covered wings. Hummingbirds flap their wings so fast that they can hover in mid-air while drinking nectar from flowers. They need a lot of control to hover – feathers make this possible.

Tail feathers help a hummingbird balance in an upright position.

Wild Turkeys

On Display

Wild turkeys are not good fliers, and domestic turkeys are often too heavy to get off the ground at all. But turkeys can still put their tail feathers to good use. A male turkey spreads its tail feathers into a fan to attract a female.

Are There Different Kinds of Feather?

A bird has several different types of feather. Each type of feather is designed for a particular purpose. Feathers vary in size and shape depending on their purpose.

Contour feathers give a bird a streamlined shape.

Tail feathers are long and straight. They are used for steering.

Flight feathers spread out at the tips.

Contour Feathers

The short feathers on a bird's head, neck, back and front are called *contour feathers*. Contour feathers give a bird a smooth shape, so it can fly easily through the air.

Birds use their beaks to keep their feathers in position.

Eider Duck

Coal Tit

Domestic Chick

Soft Down

Chicks are covered in feathers called *down*. Down feathers are very soft and fluffy. Their only purpose is to keep birds warm. Adult birds often have down mixed in with their other feathers.

Wings Feathers

There are two types of wing feather: large flight feathers and smaller feathers called *coverts*. Flight feathers make up the main surface of the wing. Covert feathers make a rounded shape at the front edge of each wing.

DID YOU KNOW?

Some birds, such as the Mallee fowl, hatch with all their feathers. They can fly within a few hours of birth.

A feather lasts for about one year. Then, it falls out and is replaced by a new one.

Covert feathers are curved to increase the thickness of the wing.

FASCINATING FEATHERY FACT

In between their other feathers, birds have tiny, hair-like bristles called *filoplumes*. These are very sensitive, and they tell a bird when its feathers need to be tidied.

What Are Feathers Made From?

The central shaft of a feather is hollow. This makes it light.

Feathers are made from a non-living substance called *keratin*. This is the same material that makes up hair, fingernails and the scales of reptiles. Different feathers have different structures, depending on their use.

The surface of a feather is made from long, narrow barbs that are zipped together.

Feathers grow from tiny holes, called *follicles*, in the surface of the skin.

Feather Structure

Every feather has a central shaft that divides it in two. Each side is called a *vane*. The outer vane of a flight feather, which faces towards the wind, is usually narrower than the inner vane. The outer edge of the feather curves steeply downwards, while the inner edge curves gently upwards.

This photograph shows the tip of a jay's wing feather.

Feathers In Close-Up

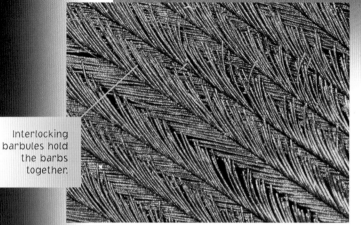

Interlocking barbules hold the barbs together.

Magnified Peacock Feather

Branching out from the central shaft are hundreds of narrow, hair-like barbs. Each barb has lots of tiny barbs, called *barbules*, branching off it. The barbules lock in with each other, fastening the barbs together. This makes the feathers strong.

Down Feathers

Down feathers do not need to be strong because their only purpose is to provide warmth. So, the shaft of a down feather is more flexible than a flight feather. Also, the barbs that make up the vanes do not zip together.

Down Feathers

Jay Feather

FASCINATING FEATHERY FACT

Before modern pens were invented, people used the shafts of feathers, dipped in ink, to write with. These were called *quills*.

How Do Birds Stay Warm?

Birds produce their own body heat. They use their feathers to stop this heat escaping. A coat of feathers provides a layer of insulation to keep birds at just the right temperature.

Heat Control

A bird's body temperature is usually warmer than the surrounding air. A layer of feathers prevents the bird from losing this heat. Feathers also provide shade and protect the bird's skin from the harmful rays of the sun.

Covert feathers can be fluffed up in cold weather. Flight feathers always remain flat.

Flamingo

Pied Wagtail

FASCINATING FEATHERY FACTS

A bird's feathers make up almost 20 percent of its total weight.

The average body temperature of a bird is about 43°C (110°F). A human being's is 37°C (98.6°F).

Fluffed Up

Feathers trap warm air between them. Down feathers are very fluffy. This means that they trap lots of air, making them warmer. When it is cold, birds can make their feathers stand on end so that even more air is trapped.

The pied wagtail fluffs up its feathers for warmth.

DID YOU KNOW?

Flamingos eat tiny shrimp that are too small to see. These shrimp give the flamingo its pink colour.

Black Grouse

Snowy Home

Thanks to a layer of feathery insulation, birds like this black grouse can live on the ground even when it is covered with snow. Underneath its feathers, the grouse's body is much warmer than its frozen surroundings.

How Do Birds Fly?

A bird flies by flapping its wings. It pushes down on the air to lift its body. With each stroke, a bird changes the position of its flight feathers. This helps it fly.

Covert feathers make the front edge of the wing rounder and thicker, giving extra lift.

FASCINATING FEATHERY FACT ·

A peregrine falcon can spot a pigeon at a distance of more than 8 km (5 miles).

Forward Flight

The wings of the peregrine falcon above are near the bottom of the down-stroke. The flight feathers are held flat as the wings push the air down and back. Air flows over the surface of the wing and creates a force that stops the bird from falling. This force is called *lift*.

Coal Tit

In order to slow down, the bird stretches its wings right back. It begins to lose its speed.

Peregrine Falcon

The eagle's wings are kept outstretched to get maximum lift while soaring.

Bald Eagle

Soaring

Birds of prey, like this bald eagle, need only flap their wings occasionally to stay high in the air. Their large wings catch currents of warm air rising from the ground, which lift them. This type of flight is called *soaring*.

The ends of flight feathers are close together so that air cannot flow between them.

The bird's tail feathers point downwards. This helps it slow down.

The bird partly folds its wings. This acts as a brake to slow it suddenly.

Flight Control

During flight, a bird's wings provide power. Its tail is used for steering. To change direction or slow down, a bird adjusts the position of its flight feathers. This changes the shape of its wings and tail. The coal tit pictured here is slowing down to feed.

DID YOU KNOW?

The peregrine falcon is the world's fastest bird. It can reach speeds of up to 350 km/h (217 mph).

How Do Birds Keep Dry?

All birds get wet from time to time, and some birds even live in water. Feathers help keep birds dry as well as warm, even when they dive beneath the water's surface.

Warm and Dry

Birds that spend a lot of time in water, such as this mandarin duck, have a specially thick coat of down feathers that traps plenty of warm air. The trapped air helps prevent water reaching the duck's skin.

Water Repellent

Ducks and other water birds give their outer feathers a coating of waterproofing oil. This oil is produced by a gland on the bird's back, near its tail. A duck uses its beak to transfer this oil onto its feathers. Water cannot soak into the oil-coated feathers.

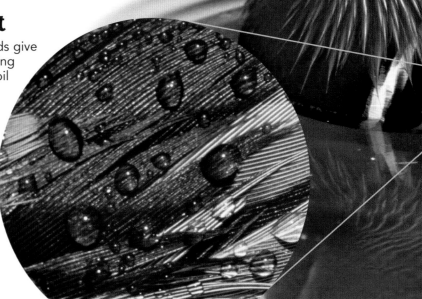

Water cannot soak between barbs that are zipped tightly together and coated with waterproof oil.

The mandarin duck has a pair of strangely shaped wing feathers called *sails*.

Mandarin Duck

FASCINATING FEATHERY FACTS

The European kingfisher usually dives no more than about 25 cm (10 inches) below the water's surface.

The emperor penguin can dive to depths of more than 250 metres (820 feet).

Bubbles of air trapped in the kingfisher's feathers give it a silvery appearance when it dives.

Kingfisher

Deep Diver

Kingfishers cannot swim on the water's surface, but they often dive under water to catch fish. Like other diving birds, they rely on their feathers to shield them from the sudden shock of cold water on their warm bodies.

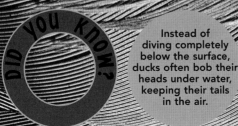

DID YOU KNOW?

Instead of diving completely below the surface, ducks often bob their heads under water, keeping their tails in the air.

What Is Preening?

Feathers need a lot of care and attention to keep them in good condition. They must be kept clean and free from parasites. Individual feathers may also need to be reshaped and repositioned. This cleaning process is called *preening*.

Guillemot

Preening Tools

The main tool a bird uses for preening is its beak, although some birds also use the claws on their feet. Beaks can grip individual feathers and pull them into the correct positions.

Did you know?

Some birds take baths on ant-hills. Ants produce a poison that kills any parasites in a birds' feathers.

When the American blue jay loses its feathers, it picks up ants and places them on its wings. The ants help soothe its skin.

A bird uses its beak to zip together any barbs that have become separated.

Oil Spills

Seabirds are in danger from oil spills at sea. The oil floats on the surface and forms an *oil slick*. To some diving birds, an oil slick can look just like a large shoal of fish. The birds dive straight through the slick and their feathers become coated with the thick oil.

Flight and tail feathers are easily moved out of place by the wind during flight, or by impact when landing.

Swan

A swan's long, bendy neck allows it to reach all of its feathers with its beak.

FASCINATING FEATHERY FACTS

The whistling swan has 25,000 feathers – more than any other bird.

Hummingbirds are so small that they have very few feathers. One species has just 940.

The feathers on the sides of the swan's body are likely to be knocked out of place. They will require lots of preening.

Lilac-Breasted Roller

Bird Baths

Some birds wash by splashing around in shallow water. Others roll around in patches of sand or dust. This rubs any parasites or pieces of dirt out of their feathers.

Are Birds Good Parents?

Young birds need a lot of care and attention from their parents. This care starts as soon as eggs are laid, and it lasts for up to a year after baby birds hatch.

Under its feathers, a bird has an area of bare skin called a *brood patch*. This is used to keep eggs and chicks warm.

Soft down feathers make a good nest lining, but eggs also need the heat of an adult duck's body to keep them warm.

Duck Nest

DID YOU KNOW?

Eagles build the biggest nests of any bird. One nest in the U.S.A. weighed more than 2 tonnes.

Feathered Nest

Some birds build elaborate nests in the trees, while others have simple hollows in the ground. The eider duck, which lives in cold regions, lines its nest with feathers from its own body. These feathers keep its eggs warm.

Bird eggs often have patterned shells. This disguises them and confuses egg thieves.

The weaver bird builds its nest by sewing leaves together with its beak.

Great Grey Owl and Owlets

Male emperor penguins huddle in groups with other males for extra warmth.

Emperor Penguins

Busy Parents

Most chicks cannot produce enough heat to keep themselves warm for long periods of time, so they stay close to their parents. Keeping eggs and chicks warm is known as *brooding*. Chicks also have to be fed and cleaned, and parents have to keep a look out for attackers that might eat the chicks.

Chicks are covered with fluffy down.

Male Warmth

Male emperor penguins look after the eggs. Each female lays a single egg onto the ice. The male puts his feet under the egg. He keeps it warmly tucked away under his brood patch. The male emperor penguin does not eat for several weeks while he cares for the egg.

Do Feathers Make Good Camouflage?

Feathers come in many different colours. Most birds have feathers that are brown or grey so they blend in with their surroundings. Both predators and prey use their feathers to conceal themselves.

These owl feathers are a dull brown, so it is easy for the owl to hide.

Short-Eared Owl Feathers

Silent Wings

Owls have the unusual ability to fly silently – their wings make no sound as they flap through the air. This means that prey cannot hear an owl approaching. It also allows the owl to hear the slightest rustle made by its prey as it scampers over the ground.

Camouflage Feathers

Owls hunt at night. During the day, they stay on the ground or perch on tree branches. These owl feathers have patches of light and dark brown that make the bird very difficult to see against bushes or tree bark. This is called *camouflage*.

FASCINATING FEATHERY FACTS ·

Soft feathers give an owl a blurred outline so it is difficult to see at night.

Owls can see very well in the dark, but they rely mainly on their hearing when hunting.

Soft fringes on the edges of an owl's feathers reduce noise.

Barn Owl

Soft feathers on an owl's legs help it move quietly.

DID YOU KNOW?

Some birds change their feathers to match the season. The ptarmigan is white in winter and brown in summer.

The colourful feathers of tropical birds help them hide from predators among flowers or brightly coloured fruit.

Safe Hiding

Most birds cannot fight off attackers, so they rely on their feathers to keep them safely hidden when danger threatens. The bittern lives among tall reeds. Stripes of coloured feathers along its body allow it to hide among the reeds.

When frightened, a bittern stands upright so that the stripes on its body line up with the reed stems.

Little Bittern

Do Feathers Send Messages?

Birds use their feathers to communicate. They send messages to other birds. Male birds usually have the biggest and brightest feathers. They use their feathers to attract females and impress rival males.

Feather Crests

Most birds have very short feathers on their heads, because longer feathers would interfere with flying and feeding. But the sulphur-crested cockatoo has a line of long, yellow feathers along the top of its head. These normally lie flat, but when the bird wants to be noticed, it lifts them into an impressive crest.

Sulphur-Crested Cockatoo

FASCINATING FEATHERY FACTS ·

A peacock's tail fan can measure 3 metres (10 feet) across.

Peacocks rattle their tail feathers together to produce an eerie shivering sound that frightens attackers.

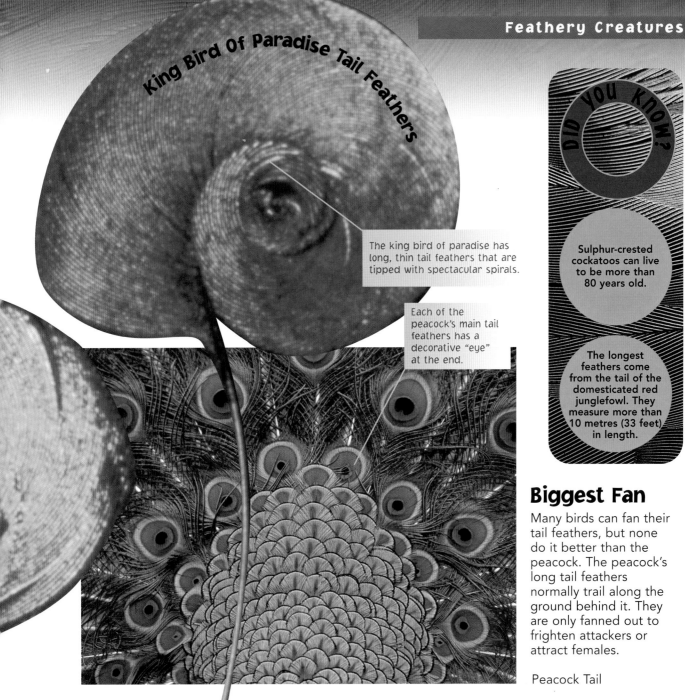

King Bird Of Paradise Tail Feathers

The king bird of paradise has long, thin tail feathers that are tipped with spectacular spirals.

Each of the peacock's main tail feathers has a decorative "eye" at the end.

DID YOU KNOW?

Sulphur-crested cockatoos can live to be more than 80 years old.

The longest feathers come from the tail of the domesticated red junglefowl. They measure more than 10 metres (33 feet) in length.

Biggest Fan

Many birds can fan their tail feathers, but none do it better than the peacock. The peacock's long tail feathers normally trail along the ground behind it. They are only fanned out to frighten attackers or attract females.

Peacock Tail

Glossary

Barbs
Small, hair-like branches that make up the vanes of a feather.

Barbules
The small hooks that zip together the barbs of a feather.

Brooding
The care and attention given to eggs and baby birds by their parents – most importantly, keeping them warm.

Camouflage
Colouration or patterns that help an animal blend in with its surroundings. This makes it hard for attackers to see the animal.

Contour Feathers
The short feathers that cover a bird's head and body. The main purpose of contour feathers is to give the bird a smooth shape.

Covert Feathers
The feathers that cover the bases of the flight feathers in the wings and tail.

Domesticated
Describes plants and animals that have been changed to suit human requirements.

Down
The short, fluffy feathers that cover the bodies of young birds. They are also found beneath the contour feathers of adults.

Flight Feathers
The long, strong feathers that cover most of a bird's wings and tail.

Insulation
A substance that reduces the amount of body heat that is lost.

Lift
The force that helps a bird fly.

Parasite

An animal or plant that lives and feeds on the body of another living thing.

Predator

Any animal that hunts and eats other animals.

Preening

The cleaning and care of feathers.

Prey

Any animal that is hunted and eaten by others.

Shaft

The long, hollow, central part of a feather. This is also sometimes called the quill.

Skin

The soft, stretchy substance that covers the bodies of animals. Skin is usually protected by fur, feathers, scales or slime.

Soaring

A type of flight in which warm air currents rising from the ground provide lift.

Vane

One of the flat side parts of a feather. A vane is made up of barbs that are zipped together.

Index